The Codependency Journal

THE
CODEPENDENCY
JOURNAL

PROMPTS AND EXERCISES TO
BUILD AND MAINTAIN
YOUR INDEPENDENCE

Kimberly Hinman, PhD

ROCKRIDGE
PRESS

First Rockridge Press trade paperback edition 2022

Rockridge Press and the Rockridge Press logo are trademarks or registered trademarks of Callisto Media Inc. and/or its affiliates in the United States and other countries and may not be used without written permission.

For general information on our other products and services, please contact our Customer Care Department within the United States at (866) 744-2665, or outside the United States at (510) 253-0500.

Paperback ISBN: 978-1-68539-723-4

Manufactured in the United States of America

Interior and Cover Designer: Regina Stadnik
Art Producer: Cristina Coppin
Editor: Adrian Potts
Production Editor: Ellina Litmanovich
Production Manager: David Zapanta

Author photo courtesy of Anna Petrow

10 9 8 7 6 5 4 3 2 1 0

This Journal Belongs To:

Contents

Introduction

Welcome to *The Codependency Journal*—a place to explore codependent traits and behaviors that make it harder to grow within yourself and your relationships with others. As someone who has personally struggled with codependency, and as a clinical psychologist working to help others understand and overcome codependency, this topic is near and dear to my heart.

Codependency refers to a relationship in which someone loses their sense of independence and believes they need to sacrifice their own needs and well-being for those of another person. It develops in childhood, when we start forming coping strategies we use throughout life to survive and manage obstacles. Codependent traits help us cope in the presence of environmental stressors and when our personal identity is somehow blocked, delayed, or otherwise disturbed. Instead of developing a clear identity and self-worth from within, life events can cause us to seek validation from the world around us.

For example, say you grew up in a tumultuous household due to high conflict or a family member's mental illness. Instead of focusing on understanding yourself, you may have coped by focusing outward to understand your environment as a means of survival. Such an environment can cause one to misinterpret their own needs as selfish, which later causes difficulty identifying and asserting personal needs and boundaries with others.

One primary treatment of codependency is cognitive behavioral therapy (CBT), which is the guiding approach of this journal. CBT frames mental health and dysfunction through the interplay of thoughts, feelings, and behaviors—meaning they all depend on and influence one another. CBT can help identify specific thoughts and feelings that fuel codependent behaviors. While understanding the past is important, the focus of CBT is on how current thoughts, feelings, and behaviors impact us today.

A journal is a great way to work through complicated emotions, but any feelings of depression or anxiety that interfere with daily life should be addressed by a medical professional. This book is not a replacement for a therapist, medication, or medical treatment. It is important to remember that at one point in your life these codependent behaviors were coping strategies that developed out of necessity to help you survive. This journal will help you abandon old behaviors that are no longer helpful and embrace new coping strategies for a life of balance and stability.

How to Use This Book

This journal is a companion to *The Codependency Workbook* by Krystal Mazzola, MEd, LMFT, and it can be used on its own or in conjunction with that book. It's divided into six sections that cover various topics related to codependency. Within each you will find a brief introduction to lay the groundwork for what you can expect, along with prompts, exercises, practices, and affirmations. The affirmations are statements you can read and repeat to yourself to combat negative thoughts, focus your mind, or find a moment of peace. The prompts are questions or statements meant to trigger exploration and introspection, and you will find space to write your thoughts after each prompt. Practices are recommended activities to add to your life and routine to aid in the healing process of unlearning codependency. The exercises span a variety of formats, such as checklists, charts, and quizzes, that allow you to further explore each topic with a more structured activity.

You can use this journal however you like. You can start at section 1 and work your way to section 6 or pick up somewhere in the middle and jump around depending on your needs or interests. Each section has its own inherent value, and the sections together provide a holistic exploration of codependency and coping strategies to manage codependency. While consistency is encouraged, as it aids in forming new habits, take to this journal at your own pace and feel no need to rush through the sections that follow.

Section 1
Set Your Goals

*When I first meet with a client, I ask them how they would know if ther-
apy had been a success. What would look different in their lives or how
might their emotions have changed? This first section is meant to do
the same. I encourage you to set goals and intentions for your journey
through* The Codependency Journal. *How do you imagine your life
looking different after completing this journal? Many times, clients will
say they want to feel less distressed, or they want to better manage
their stress. As a clinical psychologist, my goal is to help increase
my clients' insight and awareness into their thoughts, emotions, and
behaviors so they can feel more in control of themselves and less reactive to their environment. This is particularly important when working
with codependent individuals who likely learned to dismiss and
suppress their awareness of their own needs, wants, and emotions.*

Self-care is not selfish. I cannot give to others without giving first to myself.

Self-Worth Meditation

Meditation is a helpful way to slow down and recenter ourselves. Use this meditation to remind yourself that you are worthy and deserving.

1. Find a comfortable seat in a quiet place where you won't be disturbed.

2. Connect with your breath by placing a hand on your lower abdomen. Notice how it rises and falls with each breath.

3. With each breath, breathe in the words "I am deserving of," and on your exhale name a trait or sentiment you deserve. Here are some examples:

   - Breathe in, "I am deserving of," breathe out, "love."
   - Breathe in, "I am deserving of," breathe out, "kindness."
   - Breathe in, "I am deserving of," breathe out, "comfort."

Return to this practice regularly and whenever you need a reminder of your self-worth.

Codependent relationships prevent individuality. Instead, they are characterized by overlapping emotions that are indistinct from person to person; if your partner is upset, you also feel responsible to be upset. Explore moments in your life when this dynamic was at play. What are your goals for emotional boundaries in relationships moving forward?

_____

_____

_____

_____

_____

_____

_____

_____

_____

_____

_____

_____

_____

_____

_____

Codependency forms when we struggle to gauge our own needs and desires because we have learned to prioritize the needs of others. Over time this leads to resentment, anxiety, and depression. In what ways do you deny your own needs? What are your goals for recognizing and prioritizing your needs?

_____

_____

_____

_____

_____

_____

_____

_____

_____

_____

_____

_____

_____

_____

_____

_____

_____

_____

Knowing My Needs

It's time to train your brain to focus on your needs. Find some quiet time each day to ask yourself the following questions to reflect on your immediate and long-term needs.

1. What do I need right now?

2. What do I need to support myself today?

3. What do I need to support myself this week?

4. What do I need to support my relationships?

5. What do I need to support my life?

Remember, it's okay if this practice feels uncomfortable at first; over time, these questions will feel like a natural way of checking in with yourself, just as you check in with others. If discomfort arises, return to focusing on your breath to ground yourself. (Skip ahead to section 6, which begins on page 101, for some examples.)

Codependency in relationships is often characterized by one person overfunctioning and another person underfunctioning. In essence, one person is taking on full responsibility for managing the relationship. How do you see this dynamic play out in your relationships? What are your goals for a balanced relationship?

_____

_____

_____

_____

_____

_____

_____

_____

_____

_____

_____

_____

_____

_____

_____

_____

OVERFUNCTIONING CHECKLIST

Overfunctioning is characterized by blurry boundaries and investment in others' needs and outcomes to the detriment of your own. How many overfunctioning traits do you check off?

☐ I feel urgency to solve a loved one's problem.

☐ I do more than my share in relationships, so sometimes I feel exhausted or resentful.

☐ I jump in to help someone solve a problem even if they did not ask.

☐ Another person's pain and discomfort make me so uncomfortable I need to do something about it.

☐ I struggle to trust others to resolve issues without me.

☐ I identify as a caretaker in my relationships.

☐ I don't like to ask for help.

☐ I want to please everyone.

☐ I sacrifice my own needs to attend to others.

☐ I feel anxious or guilty when those close to me are upset (even if not about me).

If you ticked numerous boxes, it's likely you struggle with overfunctioning. Through this journal, you can identify and prevent overfunctioning and learn to cope by allowing others to step in and support you.

Individual perception varies depending on attitudes, beliefs, and past experiences. In codependency, you may be biased to perceive situations through the lens of abandonment, maintained by the belief that you are unworthy of love. How does fear of abandonment drive your behavior and cloud your perception? Explore the ways your perception might change if this fear didn't exist.

Conflict is natural in relationships as a way of communicating boundaries and needs. Perhaps conflict arises after one person feels neglected or overlooked. Explore the ways you communicate your needs/boundaries and accept another person's needs/boundaries. What are your goals for communication during conflicts?

_____

_____

_____

_____

_____

_____

_____

_____

_____

_____

_____

_____

_____

_____

_____

_____

When we feel unworthy, we cling to others for approval. Our actions become attempts to manipulate or control how others view us out of desperation to feel worthy. In our attempts to control others, we can inadvertently push them away. How has this dynamic played out in your life? How do you want to change it?

_____

_____

_____

_____

_____

_____

_____

_____

_____

_____

_____

_____

_____

_____

_____

_____

SELF-WORTH QUESTIONNAIRE

These prompts will help you explore how well you value yourself and your comfort asserting yourself in relationships. Rate the following statements from 0 (strongly disagree) to 5 (strongly agree).

1. I use indirect or evasive communication to avoid conflict or confrontation.   0 1 2 3 4 5

2. I have difficulty identifying what I am feeling.   0 1 2 3 4 5

3. I have difficulty making decisions independently.   0 1 2 3 4 5

4. I am embarrassed to receive recognition, praise, or gifts.   0 1 2 3 4 5

5. I prioritize others' approval of my thinking, feelings, and behavior over my own.   0 1 2 3 4 5

6. I compromise my values and integrity to avoid rejection and other people's anger.   0 1 2 3 4 5

7. I am very sensitive to others' feelings and take on their emotions.   0 1 2 3 4 5

8. I put aside my own interests to do what others want.   0 1 2 3 4 5

9. I become resentful when others decline my help or reject my advice.   0 1 2 3 4 5

10. I use lavish gifts and favors to influence others' opinions of me.   0 1 2 3 4 5

Now add up your scores:

0 to 10: You are confident and know your self-worth independent of others' opinions. Keep up the great work to further empower yourself and others.

11 to 20: You've done a lot of work to build up your sense of self and feel confident in who you are. There are just a few stones left unturned to continue the journey toward your best self.

21 to 30: You are comfortable asserting yourself in some areas but still struggle in others. You've already done a lot of the hard work. Let's use the skills you've already developed to continue to journey toward self-empowerment.

31 to 40: There have been times when you have lost yourself in relationships with others. Let's keep building on your self-awareness to foster greater authenticity.

41 to 50: It's been hard to find yourself and your voice, and you often compromise your needs in relationships. Let's start creating a genuine foundation for strong relationships with both yourself and others that will last.

Codependency is based on the faulty beliefs that you are inherently unworthy and must earn and secure attention and validation from others. Acknowledging and accepting that our beliefs are not fact is necessary to healing. Explore the origins of faulty beliefs you hold and your goals for changing your self-perception.

_____

_____

_____

_____

_____

_____

_____

_____

_____

_____

_____

_____

_____

_____

_____

_____

_____

How does your gender play a role in your perception of yourself? What have you observed about gender roles in relationships and society at large? Does this limit your view of yourself and what makes you worthy? Use the space below to explore how gender plays a role in your codependency and your goals for change.

_____

_____

_____

_____

_____

_____

_____

_____

_____

_____

_____

_____

_____

_____

_____

_____

_____

WEEKLY GOALS CALENDAR

Pick a new goal for working through codependency each week and use the calendar below to identify one thing you did each day to help you reach your goal.

	EXAMPLE GOAL: RESIST THE URGE TO FIX OTHERS' PROBLEMS.	WEEK 1 GOAL:	WEEK 2 GOAL:
MONDAY	*I wanted to fix my partner's job stress. I validated concerns instead.*		
TUESDAY	*I recognized my partner's anxiety was not mine to solve.*		
WEDNESDAY	*I told my friend, "I hear how hard this is for you."*		
THURSDAY	*I reminded myself that it's okay for others to be upset.*		
FRIDAY	*I gave my partner space to cool down when they were upset.*		
SATURDAY	*I reminded myself sometimes there aren't immediate solutions to problems.*		
SUNDAY	*My child was upset. I validated their sadness.*		

How does codependency show up in your work relationships and dynamics with co-workers? What are your goals for how you would like to challenge codependent behaviors in the workplace?

_____

_____

_____

_____

_____

_____

_____

_____

_____

_____

_____

_____

_____

_____

_____

_____

INTENTIONAL YOGA FOR SELF-COMPASSION

Yoga is a wonderful way to tap into self-compassion by challenging yourself physically and giving yourself space to make mistakes without criticism or judgment.

New and experienced yogis alike can benefit from this practice. The next time you take out your mat, take time to set your intention to be compassionate and nonjudgmental during the practice. With each pose you have the opportunity to ask yourself:

- Do I need a moment of rest? Would a child's pose serve me right now?

- Do I feel strong and want to hold the pose longer?

- Am I experiencing negative or critical thoughts to release as I exhale?

- Am I thinking in "shoulds," and are there expectations of myself and my body to release?

IDENTIFYING MY GOALS

As you near the end of the first section in *The Codependency Journal*, identify your specific goals for this journey ahead. In the following table, identify your goals, what changes you need to make to meet those goals, and the need reflected by the goal.

MY GOALS	WHAT NEEDS TO CHANGE?	MY NEEDS
Example: To feel secure being independent in my relationships.	*I need to notice and challenge my beliefs of unworthiness and practice choosing to do things on my own.*	*I need to feel authentic and secure within myself; I cannot depend on others to make me feel this way.*

Section 2
Challenge and Replace Your Negative Thoughts

Thoughts, feelings, and behaviors are intertwined into what Aaron Beck, founder of cognitive behavioral therapy, calls the "cognitive triangle"—meaning they all influence one another. If we are feeling down, we are likely to have thoughts that are more depressive, perhaps our behavior is more withdrawn, and the cycle of depression continues as each side of the triangle influences its adjacent sides. Luckily, learning to challenge and replace negative thoughts influences emotions and changes behaviors. Anyone can experience intrusive or automatic negative thoughts that disrupt daily routines. In codependent relationships, negative thoughts manifest in concerns about one's partner and interfere with activities that are important to you. This section explores the origins of your negative thoughts and provides specific strategies for challenging your negative thoughts and replacing them with more adaptive and healthy thoughts.

Today, I
give myself
permission
to be greater
than my fears.

Concerns about a relationship's sustainability are normal. However, too many negative thoughts cause you to lose sight of what you want from a relationship as you hyperfocus on what you don't want— rejection or abandonment. What do you want from a relationship? Shift your focus onto what you might gain, not lose.

_____

_____

_____

_____

_____

_____

_____

_____

_____

_____

_____

_____

_____

_____

_____

_____

_____

_____

Fighting the Finger Trap Exercise

Codependent intrusive thoughts are often obsessive thoughts or fears about rejection. Imagine your fingers in a finger trap—the more you pull, the harder it tightens. Similarly, the more you try to avoid intrusive thoughts, the more you become stuck in a cycle of them.

1. **Try this:** Pick a bothersome intrusive thought, and for thirty seconds, do everything possible to avoid thinking about it.

2. **How did that go?** Often, avoiding intrusive thoughts means we give them even more power.

3. **Now try this:** Repeat the same intrusive thought repeatedly in your mind for thirty seconds.

How was this? Many times, the intensity of the fearful thought lessens after repeating it to yourself for ten to fifteen seconds. Actively repeating the thought is like pushing your fingers toward each other to release the finger trap. It seems counterintuitive at first. Hopefully, you realize it isn't the thought itself but the emotions you attach to it that feel dangerous. The only way out of the intrusive thought cycle is to lean in and challenge the power of this thought over you.

Codependency causes us to believe we must perfect our roles (i.e., parent, partner, friend, coworker) to feel good about ourselves. In what ways do you experience this? How can you challenge these thoughts to see yourself more holistically?

_____

_____

_____

_____

_____

_____

_____

_____

_____

_____

_____

_____

_____

_____

_____

_____

_____

_____

_____

_____

_____

Imagine a fun-house carnival mirror that distorts your body proportions. Despite not having these proportions, this is what the mirror shows. Similarly, cognitive distortions distort reality.

One distortion is all-or-nothing thinking. In other words, you perceive things in terms of extremes—something is either wonderful or terrible, you are either perfect or a failure. By becoming aware of these thoughts, it's possible to restructure them to find more nuance—as the truth often lies somewhere in the middle. Use the following table to try this now. Read the example, then write how this type of thinking might happen in your life and try restructuring it.

ALL-OR-NOTHING THOUGHT	RESTRUCTURED THOUGHT
Example: "I always care for people, and they never show up for me."	*"I enjoy showing up for others and sometimes life circumstances prevent them from doing the same."*

Another distortion is catastrophizing, or exaggerating thoughts to assume the worst. By becoming aware of this thinking, it's possible to stop your thoughts from escalating and stay grounded in reality. Use the table to try restructuring one of these thoughts.

CATASTROPHIZING THOUGHT	RESTRUCTURED THOUGHT
Example: "Others will judge me if I tell them how I really feel and I won't be able to handle that."	*"It's scary to let others know how I feel, and I can tolerate the anxiety in order to form authentic relationships."*

Intrusive thoughts stem from difficulty tolerating distressing emotions and from learning to hide or ignore painful emotions instead of processing them. How do fears about relationships with others fuel your intrusive thoughts? Explore the painful emotions you hide from and see if you can release them here.

_____

_____

_____

_____

_____

_____

_____

_____

_____

_____

_____

_____

_____

_____

_____

_____

_____

Distress Tolerance

Thoughts are not actions or tangible experiences. However, we often confuse our thoughts with reality and fear they will come true. To combat intrusive thoughts, we must break the connection between thoughts and actions. Learning to sit with the distress of an uncomfortable thought instead of reacting to it weakens the intensity and power of intrusive thoughts. Try this distress tolerance practice:

Accept distressing thoughts and the emotions associated with those thoughts. Remind yourself that distress is temporary. Do not try to fight or change your emotions, as this is not true acceptance.

1. I accept my fear of _____.

2. My emotions are valid, and this experience is painful.

3. My fear of _____ happening does not mean it *will* happen.

4. If my fear does come true, I am still a worthy and lovable person.

If our thoughts leave us feeling stuck and alone, it is likely because they are too rigid and don't leave much room for other possibilities or perspectives. Use this space to explore moments you felt alone or misunderstood and look for alternative possibilities or perspectives to your previously held beliefs.

_____

_____

_____

_____

_____

_____

_____

_____

_____

_____

_____

_____

_____

_____

_____

_____

Changing behavior is another way to challenge faulty beliefs. Use the following for ideas on how to challenge faulty beliefs through action and then fill in the remaining table with your own beliefs and challenges. After you have challenged your faulty beliefs by behaving in ways that contradict them, write down your new reframed belief that is more based in reality.

FAULTY BELIEF	ACTION TO CHALLENGE THIS BELIEF	NEW REFRAMED BELIEF
"I am worthless without others."	I will spend a day by myself and practice self-affirmations of self-worth.	"Even when on my own, I am inherently worthy and do not need to earn my worth."
"I need the approval of others."	I will make a decision without seeking approval from others first.	"I know myself best and can make decisions without approval from others."
"I must be useful to others, or they will leave me."	I will resist the urge to provide acts of service to others in my relationships.	"My worth is more than my ability to provide for others."

Do you often think something like "I feel uncomfortable, but I'm worried they will push me away if I don't go"? Practice saying "and" instead of "but" to identify your concerns, while also asserting your boundaries. How often do you ignore your emotions because you fear the reactions of others? What if you validated your emotions and communicated them to others? How would your relationships change?

Use the space below write down intrusive thoughts or concerns about others that plague you. Then try flipping these by placing yourself at the center. For instance, if one of your worries is, "I need to make sure that others are enjoying themselves," you could change it to, "I need to make sure I am enjoying myself." How does this change the intensity of the thought?

_____

_____

_____

_____

_____

_____

_____

_____

_____

_____

_____

_____

_____

How does blame play a role in your relationships? How often do you blame others for your emotions or take responsibility for how others feel? What if you could take responsibility for your own emotions and no one else's?

Getting Curious

We often learn to place emotions into two categories: good and bad. Instead, try categorizing emotions as pleasant and unpleasant. Remember, emotions are tools to help you understand if your needs are being met and help you communicate your needs to others. Use this practice to become curious about your emotions without judging them.

1. *What emotion am I experiencing?* See if you can just name the emotion without trying to judge it.

2. *Where do I feel this emotion in my body?* See if you can watch the emotion move throughout your body. Perhaps it starts in your chest and radiates out from there.

3. *What is this emotion trying to communicate to me?* How is it connected to a met or unmet need?

In codependency, we can get stuck in the "fallacy of change," the belief that if we work hard enough, we can transform someone into who we want them to be. Where and when do you notice this belief in your life? How would your life be different if you acknowledge this belief is untrue?

_____

_____

_____

_____

_____

_____

_____

_____

_____

_____

_____

_____

_____

_____

_____

_____

OTHER COMMON COGNITIVE DISTORTIONS

In the following table, you will find two final common cognitive distortions. External control fallacy involves the belief that your life is controlled by external sources, such as people, events, or dynamics. By noticing this belief, you can resume control and stop feeling helpless. Write down an example of this type of thinking and then try restructuring it, as you did on page 30.

EXTERNAL CONTROL FALLACY THOUGHT	RESTRUCTURED THOUGHT
Example: "They made me feel awful about myself."	"I am responsible for my own emotions and no one else's."

The second distortion is internal control fallacy, or believing you have complete control of yourself and those around you—meaning you are responsible for the suffering or joy of those around you. By noticing this belief, you can set healthy boundaries and take responsibility for only yourself.

INTERNAL CONTROL FALLACY THOUGHT	RESTRUCTURED THOUGHT
Example: "If I make sure the house is immaculate, they won't feel stressed and start drinking."	"I cannot control their drinking habits. I do not have control over their behavior."

Progressive Muscle Relaxation

Just as we hold rigid thoughts, we hold rigidity in our bodies. This practice helps you identify tension in your body and practice letting go of that tension. As you release tension in your body, practice releasing tension in your thoughts.

1. Sit or lie down in a comfortable position.

2. Take a deep cleansing breath and hold it for a few seconds.

3. Exhale slowly and feel tension leave your body.

4. Repeat a few times.

5. Now move your attention to the tips of your toes and feet. Tense your feet by curling your toes and the arches of your feet and hold the tension for five seconds. As you release your toes, notice the new feeling of relaxation.

6. Repeat this process, moving all the way up your body, lower legs, upper legs, pelvis, etc., and end with a full-body tense and release.

Section 3
Identify Your Triggers

As you uncover your codependent habits, it is important you also learn to identify what triggers them. A trigger in codependency is anything that causes distress and, often, leads to avoidance of uncomfortable emotions. Perhaps you avoid arguments by giving in, or maybe the fear of being alone keeps you in an unfulfilling relationship. This section will help you approach triggers with caution and safely move past them.

Your triggers keep you stuck in codependency by preventing you from facing your fears. Recognizing how certain situations affect you will enable you to respond proactively instead of reactively. Let's dive in.

I will not
tiptoe around
the feelings
of others.

A common emotion in codependency is resentment, like resenting others for taking advantage or resenting how much you do for others. Work backward and journal about the causes or events that led up to your resentment. Very often, avoidance of your triggers leads to resentment. See if you can identify them.

_____

_____

_____

_____

_____

_____

_____

_____

_____

_____

_____

_____

_____

_____

_____

_____

_____

_____

Discomfort with asserting yourself and your needs is a common trigger. Explore when you've avoided asserting yourself and how you felt emotionally. What fears about asserting yourself hold you back?

_____

_____

_____

_____

_____

_____

_____

_____

_____

_____

_____

_____

_____

_____

_____

_____

_____

_____

Seeking approval is a common response to the trigger of being rejected. How often do you find yourself seeking approval from coworkers or managers? Explore how much workplace enjoyment depends on achieving approval from others? What might it feel like to give this approval to yourself and not rely on coworkers?

Exposure therapy should include grounding/relaxation tools that you feel comfortable using, like deep belly breathing or visualizing candle wax slowly dripping down a burning candle. Whatever they are, practice them regularly before trying exposure therapy for best results.

First, identify a trigger—for instance, a parent from whom you are estranged. Now imagine something related to that trigger that would bring about the most distress for you, a 10/10. For instance, the thought of going away on a family vacation with your parent. Write this on the top rung of the ladder on the next page.

Now choose a situation that is a 5/10—moderately distressing but not nearly as bad as the previous situation. For instance, you might imagine having a ten-minute phone call with your parent.

Work your way up or down from there by filling in the remaining rungs of the ladder. Remember, the bottom rung is a 1/10, something that requires minimal coping and is relatively stress-free.

Begin your exposure therapy with the first rung on the ladder, perhaps simply visualizing talking to your parent or sending an email to them. Pair this exposure with your grounding technique. You're ready to move on if your distress stays below a 4 out of 10. The goal isn't 0 out of 10—this is unrealistic, and you want to minimize and contain anxiety, not to completely erase it. Anxiety might not be reduced right away in each step, and that's okay. Remember, for this to work, you need to retrain your brain to associate the trigger with relaxation and grounding instead of distress.

10	_____
9	_____
8	_____
7	_____
6	_____
5	_____
4	_____
3	_____
2	_____
1	_____

What are your triggers? How do you currently respond and how can you respond more proactively?

TRIGGER	CURRENT RESPONSE	NEW RESPONSE
Needing to say "no."	*Worry that others will be offended and I will harm the relationship, so I overextend myself.*	*Set boundaries and challenge irrational thoughts.* *Example: "I can't today. I hope it goes well."*

Exposure therapy slowly exposes you to a trigger and includes relaxation techniques to train your brain to respond differently to the trigger. The first step to doing this is imaginal exposure—imagining your trigger in detail. Use the space below to write about a triggering experience. As you write, take pauses for deep breathing, repeating affirmations, and other grounding exercises. Make sure your anxiety stays below a 4 out of 10 as you do this.

Five Questions to De-Catastrophize

Next time you experience a trigger of codependency, ask yourself the following questions to de-catastrophize and think more clearly.

1. **If my worst-case fear comes true, what will happen?** Example: "I tell my partner to start paying their portion of the rent, they break up with me, and will be alone."

2. **How likely is it that the worst-case scenario will happen on a scale of 1 (highly unlikely) to 5 (highly likely)?** Example: "It's a 3, as it's possible, but it's more likely that they will be upset and eventually cool down."

3. **How much distress will I feel if this happens on a scale of 1 (no distress) to 5 (total distress)?** Example: "It's an 4—this will be painful at first; I have talked with family and friends to help me through the pain."

4. **How much will this matter to me in one hour? One week? One month? One year?** Example: "The first hour will be the worst and will lessen over weeks and months. In a year I'll likely no longer be in distress."

5. **Can I manage the distress for the length of time this will realistically affect me?** Example: "Yes, I can see my therapist and use coping skills to manage the initial intensity of the distress, and it will fade over time."

Many triggers of codependency stem from a poor understanding of oneself, which can lead to difficulty finding meaning and purpose. People with codependency attach meaning to their connections, while conflating losing those connections with losing one's purpose or meaning. Use this space to explore this notion and how it shows up in your life.

Feeling emotions that have long been suppressed can initially be scary. To avoid this, we might unconsciously seek out individuals with big emotions for us to focus on and attend to, thereby allowing us to neglect ourselves further. Explore how you avoid caring for your emotional needs and whether self-compassion might be triggering for you.

Have a Conversation with Yourself

As you continue to explore and challenge your triggers, it is important to pair this exploration with self-compassion. Shame makes us turn away from and dismiss our emotions; compassion helps us turn toward our pain with openness and acceptance.

Practice having a conversation with yourself using these phrases. Come back to this practice regularly and whenever you need an extra dose of self-compassion.

- I know you are struggling, and I am here for you.

- I want to support you any way I can.

- You are doing your best, and I see that.

- You are not alone in this.

Take this scenario of Alex and Sam. Alex learned that Sam had been unfaithful again despite previous promises to change. Alex felt triggered by emotions of abandonment and loneliness and, in response, latched tighter to the relationship, requesting access to Sam's phone and calling or texting incessantly when they were apart. Alex thought maybe she could prevent Sam's cheating by keeping a closer eye on Sam. Instead, this pushed Sam further away. Sam resented Alex's controlling and jealous behavior, and eventually Sam and Alex ended their relationship in a painful and contentious breakup.

Now it's your turn. Rewrite the above scenario taking on the role of Alex. Try to empathize and use compassion toward Alex and provide an alternative way of responding to Sam's infidelities. Use the skills from earlier in the section to identify healthy boundaries and responses Alex could use when confronting Sam.

UNHEALTHY THOUGHTS/ BEHAVIORS	NEW THOUGHT	NEW RESPONSE
Example: Alex feels abandoned, so she tries to control Sam's behavior to prevent herself from being hurt.	*"It is acceptable to want my partner to be faithful. I cannot control their actions. I can only control my own."*	*Alex asks Sam for a break from the relationship so she can take time to care for herself and reinforce that she will not accept Sam's behavior.*

Codependency often includes excusing others' behavior. Perhaps your partner stayed out late and is too hungover to make it to brunch with your family and you find yourself rationalizing that they deserved a night out because they work so hard. Use the space below to recall occasions when you rationalized others' behavior because you wanted to avoid feeling hurt. Now practice acknowledging and accepting the hurt you feel. How might you communicate your emotions to the person whose actions were hurtful to you?

CHALLENGING REINFORCEMENTS FOR TRIGGERS

We reinforce triggers with our thoughts and behaviors. For instance, you respond to a situation with anxiety, and you reinforce this anxiety with thoughts that encourage you to feel more anxious, or you behave in ways that make anxiety worse. In the following table, explore how your thoughts and behaviors reinforce your triggers and identify challenges to your thoughts and alternative behaviors to diminish the strength of your triggers.

	EXAMPLE	CHALLENGING MY TRIGGER 1	CHALLENGING MY TRIGGER 2
SITUATION	My partner keeps making comments to me about how attractive other people are.		
TRIGGER	Feeling unworthy, not good enough, fear they will leave me.		
OLD THOUGHT	"I need to dress better so I can keep their attention."		
NEW THOUGHT	"It's acceptable for me to ask my partner not to comment on the appearance of others."		
OLD BEHAVIOR	Strict dieting and overexercising.		
NEW BEHAVIOR	Loving-kindness meditation and yoga practice.		

How does guilt show up in your life? How often do you feel guilty and in what contexts? Unhealthy guilt usually stems from rigid beliefs or expectations about yourself. Use the space below to challenge rigid beliefs that lead to unhealthy guilt. What is the evidence for these beliefs? How are they limiting you?

_____

_____

_____

_____

_____

_____

_____

_____

_____

_____

_____

_____

_____

_____

_____

_____

Differentiating Healthy vs. Unhealthy Guilt

Boundaries are difficult without a plan to manage guilt. When we first establish boundaries with individuals with whom we're codependent, it can lead to overwhelming guilt that tempts us to compromise our needs to absolve ourselves of the guilt. Instead, try asking yourself the following questions to differentiate guilt: healthy (based on your wrong actions) versus unhealthy (based on unrealistic expectations).

1. What specifically do you think you are doing wrong?

2. Is it based on unrealistic expectations or distorted thoughts?
   - If yes, check in on rigid thinking styles and challenge irrational thoughts or expectations. Your guilt is not based in reality.
   - If no, is there room to solve a problem or change the situation to right a wrong?
     - If no, return to self-compassion and remind yourself you are trying the best you can.

The belief that we are responsible for others' problems is a frequent trigger in codependency that leads to a "superhero syndrome" or trying to fix everyone's problems. How often are you acting like a superhero to avoid tolerating your own distress and allowing others to feel and tolerate their own?

Section 4
Problem-Solving in a Codependent Relationship

Problems related to codependency in relationships are twofold. On one side, codependency can lead individuals to stay in unhealthy relationships for longer, due to the belief that they can somehow mold the other individual into what the codependent individual wants. Separately, codependency can foster insecurity and brew problems in relationships out of fearful reactions to normal stressors in a partnership due to fears of abandonment.

This section provides an overview of how codependency frames stressful events in relationships as catastrophic and dangerous and gives you tools to reframe your perception of normal stressors in relationships. It will also help you distinguish between normal ups and downs in relationships and find ways to handle normal stressors that don't leave you vulnerable to abusive and unhealthy dynamics that result from faulty beliefs about being able to control or change your partner.

I don't have
to give
100 percent to
every person
in my life.

Are you still blaming yourself for negative life events outside your control? This may have been an adaptive strategy in childhood, but now you are an adult with agency, and this belief is no longer helpful. Explore how you continue to hold maladaptive beliefs. As you work to release these beliefs, thank them for once serving and protecting you and explore the ways in which they no longer help but harm.

_____

_____

_____

_____

_____

_____

_____

_____

_____

_____

_____

_____

_____

_____

_____

_____

_____

How do you make decisions? Codependency clouds your sense of self, which makes it harder to feel empowered to make decisions. Reflect on how it would feel to make a decision without consulting others. How would it feel to identify and accept your own needs and desires before those of others?

_____

_____

_____

_____

_____

_____

_____

_____

_____

_____

_____

_____

_____

_____

_____

_____

_____

Many of our relationships are with coworkers or clients we work with. How do you problem solve conflicts in the workplace? If there is any difference in how you problem solve issues in your personal life compared to work life? Why might this be?

_____

_____

_____

_____

_____

_____

_____

_____

_____

_____

_____

_____

_____

_____

_____

_____

_____

_____

PROBLEM-SOLVING SIMPLIFIED

Use the flowchart to help you figure out a healthy course of action for your next relationship conflict. This flowchart walks step-by-step through the process of identifying a problem and resolving it in a way that supports open communication and internal reflection.

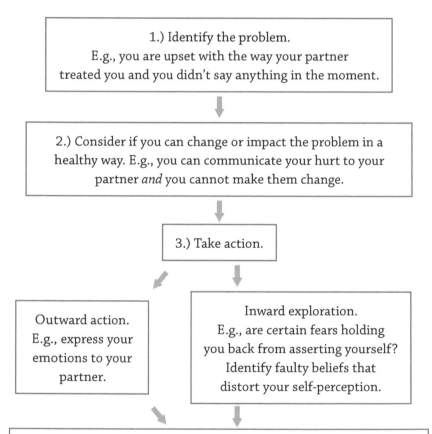

1.) Identify the problem.
E.g., you are upset with the way your partner treated you and you didn't say anything in the moment.

2.) Consider if you can change or impact the problem in a healthy way. E.g., you can communicate your hurt to your partner *and* you cannot make them change.

3.) Take action.

Outward action. E.g., express your emotions to your partner.

Inward exploration. E.g., are certain fears holding you back from asserting yourself? Identify faulty beliefs that distort your self-perception.

4) Acceptance. Once you've acted outwardly and/or inwardly, it's time to accept reality. Remind yourself you cannot change the reality of the situation no matter how much distress it causes you. You can choose to keep your pain temporary and prevent it from becoming suffering by accepting it and moving forward.

It can be difficult to express true feelings for fear of rejection. Finding your voice takes time. Use this space to express true feelings you have held back. The more you practice expressing these, the easier it will become to represent yourself and develop authentic, balanced relationships.

My Values Compass

Imagine you have a compass that lets you know if you're heading in a direction that is consistent with your values in life. Whether it's honesty, companionship, growth, or playfulness, only you know what really matters to you and what fills your life with meaning.

When problems arise in relationships, pull out your "compass" and question if there's a solution in alignment with your values. You might ask yourself "Can I solve this problem in a way that is consistent with my values, or is it time to walk away from the situation?" Or choose whatever wording best matches your internal compass; the goal is to take time to pause and reflect on the direction in which you're headed and make sure the destination reflects your values.

How often have you planned an entire event or outing in your mind only to feel let down when one part of the plan goes awry? Reflect on how much of this was because you assumed you could control aspects of others that were outside of your control. What if you didn't allow your mood to depend on unrealistic expectations?

_____

_____

_____

_____

_____

_____

_____

_____

_____

_____

_____

_____

_____

_____

_____

THE ROOT OF MY RELATIONSHIP PROBLEMS

This checklist provides insight to help you identify themes in the root causes of your conflicts. Check the statements that apply to your relationship.

Section A

☐ Conflicts are usually related to my fears of being abandoned or worries about being alone.

☐ I do things to keep my partner close and reduce my fear of them leaving. In disagreements, I jump to the conclusion that we'll break up or separate.

☐ I like to have events scheduled far into the future with my partner; this allows me to feel more in control of my future with them.

Section B

☐ My partner can be disrespectful at times, and I make excuses or rationalize their behavior.

☐ I often feel guilty after arguments, believing I caused the argument by upsetting my partner and should not have.

☐ Sometimes my partner's behavior scares me and I walk on eggshells to avoid upsetting them.

☐ I find myself giving my partner second chances very often.

Mostly from section A: Your relationship problems stem from fears of being neglected or rejected. To cope with this, you often use controlling tactics to avoid feeling pain. Your partner may feel overwhelmed with little room to communicate their emotional distress to you. Fortunately, you're in the right place to learn how to tolerate your partner's distress and take feedback from them without catastrophizing.

Mostly from section B: Your relationship problems stem largely from an imbalance in support and caretaking. You overextend yourself to meet the needs of your partner, and your partner may at times take advantage of your generosity. You're in the right place to learn how to stop putting others' needs before your own and subsequently putting yourself in harm's way. If you have ever experienced abuse, please contact the national hotline for domestic violence at (800) 799-7233 and see the back of the book for additional resources on page 121.

A mix of both: Your relationship problems stem from a mixture of anxiety and a desire to control the outcome of your relationship, and an imbalance in caretaking and support in which you may be taken advantage of. It is important to understand when to use self-reflection to make changes to your own behavior versus when a boundary has been crossed and you have lost yourself and your ability to care for yourself in the relationship. Keep reading to explore when problems are solvable or outside your control.

Often in a codependent relationship, when one individual is upset, the codependent individual immediately feels distressed and wants to "save" the other and fix their distress. Use the space below to imagine what it would feel like to acknowledge and validate another's emotions without needing to change them. Write about ways to tolerate others' pain without taking it on as your own.

_____

_____

_____

_____

_____

_____

_____

_____

_____

_____

_____

_____

_____

_____

_____

_____

Find Your Community to Find Yourself

Experiencing a sense of belonging and comradery leads to higher levels of self-esteem. Try joining a community group of like-minded individuals or those with whom you share similar interests. A strong sense of self and identity will strengthen your ability to set and stick with healthy boundaries in your relationship and be able to identify your wants, needs, and desires more effectively. The stronger your self-esteem, the less you will lean on your relationship to prop you up and support you.

WHAT'S MINE AND WHAT'S YOURS

Identify what you can take responsibility for and what you need to allow your partner to take responsibility for. Use the following to separate out your own contributions to arguments and conflicts and then identify how to solve these problems in the future. An example is provided.

PROBLEM	MY CONTRIBUTION	THEIR CONTRIBUTION	SOLUTION
Example: There are dirty dishes in the sink, and I am tired of always doing them.	I overextended myself and grew resentful without communicating my frustration until it spilled over.	They saw the dirty dishes and deprioritized it until after they relaxed from the day.	Create a chores chart and communicate about who does what/when and check in regularly about stress levels.

Think of a time you felt someone neglected to recognize your efforts or actions. Now think about how often you put your partner's needs above your own. Explore ways you can recognize and prioritize your own needs instead of waiting for others to do so. How can you release expectations and resentfulness of others?

_____

_____

_____

_____

_____

_____

_____

_____

_____

_____

_____

_____

_____

_____

_____

_____

_____

_____

_____

Use a recent argument to explore your mental boundaries—these protect your right to have your own thoughts, values, and opinions. Often in codependency we are easily swayed by others and have loose mental boundaries. How loose or rigid are yours? Journal about how a recent argument might look different if you set strong mental boundaries that allowed you to both hold on to your own beliefs and listen to different opinions of others, knowing they do not threaten the standing of your own opinions.

Boundaries are an important and healthy part of a successful relationship. However, if you struggle with codependency, you may wrongly worry that if your partner is setting boundaries they are rejecting or abandoning you. For instance, your partner says they had a long day and want to spend the night alone, and you interpret this as a sign that they are upset with you for something you said earlier in the day. Write about any moments you have confused your partner setting a boundary with a direct attack on you. How could you approach this differently in the future?

_____

_____

_____

_____

_____

_____

_____

_____

_____

_____

_____

_____

_____

_____

_____

_____

SECOND CHANCES

Keep track of how often you "give a second chance" to your partner. Use the following table to describe the situation and track your reasoning. Identify which of your needs are being jeopardized by the second chances, and identify when to stop. When will you say no to giving second chances? An example is provided to help start you off.

Everyone deserves an opportunity to learn from the past and try again. However, it is important to clarify for yourself how many second chances are too many. What is your own limit?

DESCRIPTION OF THE SITUATION	YOUR REASONING	WHAT NEEDS ARE BEING JEOPARDIZED?	WHAT IS YOUR TIPPING POINT?
Example: My partner is late on their portion of the rent and asked me to cover for them again this month.	*It's hard for them to find work right now. I can adjust my budget to cover their part of the rent this month.*	*My financial security, feeling supported and respected in my relationship.*	*I can't afford to keep paying both portions of rent. My partner will need to begin paying by next month.*

Explore your thoughts and feelings about the statement "I have learned to put myself down, and my behavior invites others to do the same." Giving too many second chances can be a sign that we are out of touch with our own self-worth or that it was not well established to begin with. How might you talk to a friend or loved one about the way your partner treats you? If your response to others is different from your response to yourself, why is this so?

Radical Acceptance in Everyday Life

Radical acceptance is a term that was first introduced by clinical psychologist Marsha Linehan to help individuals tolerate pain and resist the urge to try to change a situation or deny reality, which is what ultimately leads to suffering. Before we can take on radically accepting significant life events, we can practice on smaller moments that are disappointing or unpleasant but not major disturbances to our daily lives. Practicing using radical acceptance each day will allow you to use it effectively when you really need it.

1. Acknowledge the present situation without judgment or need for immediate solution.

2. Ask, "Can I control what happens?" If not, choose not to fight it, because that is a losing battle.

3. Release judgment of the situation and open your eyes to seeing things how they truly are, not how you want them to be.

4. Remind yourself that the past cannot be changed.

5. Take a few deep breaths to be present in the moment.

Where does magical thinking show up in your relationships with others? This might resemble statements such as, "If only _____ happened then I would be happy." Use the space below to identify magical thinking and challenge the belief that changing one aspect of your life would magically make your suffering disappear. How would introducing acceptance change your suffering?

Section 5

Manage Conflicts and Emotions

Conflict is a natural part of every relationship. It allows partners to communicate and acknowledge personal boundaries. Often conflict is perceived negatively and thought of as something to be avoided. Perhaps you grew up in a household with excessive conflict, and conflict brings up painful memories. Or maybe you grew up in a household where you didn't observe any conflict, and now it feels foreign to you.

This section will help you redefine your relationship with conflict. You're not meant to necessarily enjoy conflict, but you can learn how to tolerate it and understand its purpose in your relationships. This section will help you solve conflicts to better understand the root of the conflict and learn effective ways to manage it.

I am in charge
of my future;
I have all that I
need to grow.

What memories, thoughts, and feelings do you associate with conflict? Reflect on any "should" or "shouldn't" statements you hold. These are cognitive distortions that restrict your thinking. Perhaps it's "I should be easygoing" or "I shouldn't argue." Explore what it would be like to release your current expectations and open yourself up to other interpretations of conflict in relationships.

Conflict is defined as a "mental struggle resulting from incompatible or opposing needs, drives, wishes, or external or internal demands." Explore the ways in which conflict can act in service of a partnership. How could conflict help you and your partner communicate your respective needs?

_____

_____

_____

_____

_____

_____

_____

_____

_____

_____

_____

_____

_____

_____

_____

_____

_____

_____

_____

You Don't Have to Go In Alone

In codependency, the urge to perfect, control, and fix issues yourself without input from others is tempting. However, this can make others feel left in the dark, manipulated, or controlled by your attempts to fix issues.

Try asking for your partner's input in conflict instead of resolving it on your own. First, identify the problematic behavior, then ask for support in the form of brainstorming solutions together.

Here is an example to help get you started: "I've noticed we often get into arguments when you get home from work, and I want to brainstorm together about ways to change this pattern."

Now you try with your partner: "I've noticed _____, and I want to brainstorm together about ways to change this pattern."

Have conflicts arisen because you initially downplayed your needs, only allowing them to surface after exploding from the pressure of trying to ignore or suppress them? Explore what it feels like to express your needs without an explosion of emotions. Write about how you can have regular doses of conflict so you don't over-dose later.

FAST Skill

Think of a conflict you had with someone recently, and use this FAST practice to explore a new way of responding to the conflict that maintains your self-respect and personal boundaries.

Fair: How can you be fair to both yourself and others? Challenge unfair thoughts or statements, such as "They will leave me if I say no." Instead, be fair and acknowledge the needs of both yourself and the other individual.

(no) **A**pologies: No unjustified apologies welcome. Are you sorry or actually uncomfortable with someone's unpleasant emotions?

Stick to your values: Don't compromise yourself or your values to conform to the needs of others.

Truthful: Don't lie or exaggerate the truth. Sometimes we lie to try to protect someone's feelings or control the outcome of a situation. This only builds walls in relationships rather than solidifying connections.

HOW MUCH DOES CONTROL PLAY A ROLE?

The roots of codependency come from a desire for control, but we really don't have as much control over our lives as we might like to believe. Conflict can arise when we feel out of control or worry we will lose control in some way. Reflect on how much control plays a role in your relationship by completing this questionnaire. 1 = almost never, 2 = occasionally, 3 = sometimes, 4 = often, 5 = very often

1. I felt sad and worried after thinking my partner or others didn't need me, so I inserted myself in their plans. 1 2 3 4 5

2. I believed if I could change my partner to do or be what I wanted, then I would be happy. 1 2 3 4 5

3. I felt taken advantage of after I went above and beyond to help my partner with an issue they were having. 1 2 3 4 5

4. I felt pushed away after my attempts to please and accommodate my partner's needs. 1 2 3 4 5

5. I didn't trust my partner and became suspicious and jealous. 1 2 3 4 5

6. I told my partner what I thought they wanted to hear, but it wasn't what I actually felt. 1 2 3 4 5

7. I have tried to force my relationship in a direction of more commitment. 1 2 3 4 5

8. I've noticed my need for perfection or rigid thinking conflicts with reality or my partner's behaviors. 1 2 3 4 5

9. I held back emotions from my partner because I feared their response to me. 1 2 3 4 5

10. I have felt my partner's behavior reflected poorly on me. 1 2 3 4 5

Now add up your scores:

10 to 23: Need for control does not play a big role in conflicts in your relationship. Great work. You allow things to flow, generally trusting the process.

24 to 37: You're doing the work and starting to recognize that your need for control can fuel conflict in your relationship. Continue to check in with yourself about passive-aggressive tendencies, challenging yourself to be direct.

38 to 50: Your fear of losing control weighs heavily on your relationship and is a top contributor to arguments and conflicts in your relationship. The first step is confronting and accepting your need for control and challenging fears of losing it. Keep up the good work and exploration by using this workbook.

What reactions did you have to the results of the quiz on the previous page? What surprised you? Were there any "aha!" moments of recognition? It can be hard to recognize the ways in which a need for control motivates our behavior. Explore what you've uncovered about yourself as it relates to control and conflict.

_____

_____

_____

_____

_____

_____

_____

_____

_____

_____

_____

_____

_____

_____

_____

_____

Learning to be comfortable with conflict often means learning to release unrealistic expectations. How do unrealistic or rigid relationship expectations prevent you from experiencing conflict as helpful and normal? Explore the ways catastrophic thinking (i.e., assuming the worst-case scenario) is an outcome of conflict for you. What could be a different outcome?

_____

_____

_____

_____

_____

_____

_____

_____

_____

_____

_____

_____

_____

_____

_____

_____

COMMUNICATING DIRECTLY

Learning how to take responsibility for your part in a conflict is essential to arguing fairly and respecting boundaries. This can be hard to do at first if you aren't in touch with your emotional needs. Instead, you might find yourself pointing fingers at your partner and labeling their actions or emotions instead of your own. Use the following table to practice taking responsibility for your emotional needs. Pointing fingers usually involves the words "I feel that you . . ." while the important emotion underlying that statement is not communicated directly.

POINTING FINGERS	IDENTIFYING YOUR EMOTIONAL NEEDS	DEEPER EXPLORATION/ INTROSPECTION
Example: "I feel that you prioritize other things before me."	"I feel unimportant to you."	It is a fear not a fact that I am unimportant to my partner. My partner can have time to themselves and still value our time together.

Go back in time to a conflict with your partner, and this time enter with the mindset that your partner is doing the best they can and are not intentionally trying to hurt you. How does your mood or perception of the conflict change? How would a mindset of mutual goodwill change your current pattern of conflict?

_____

_____

_____

_____

_____

_____

_____

_____

_____

_____

_____

_____

_____

_____

_____

_____

KNOWING MY RIGHTS

In conflicts with others, we need to have a clear sense of our rights and how to assert and defend them. This is often difficult in co-dependency because we have not practiced seeking out and focusing on ourselves as much as on others. In the space provided, identify your rights and ways to assert them in times of conflict. The more you learn to assert yourself, the better communication you will have and the less resentful you will feel.

I have the right to _say no._

I will assert this right by _listening to my internal needs and letting go of guilt about setting boundaries._

I have the right to _____

I will assert this right by _____

_____

_____

_____

I have the right to _____

I will assert this right by _____

_____

_____

_____

I have the right to _____

I will assert this right by _____

_____

_____

_____

I have the right to _____

I will assert this right by _____

_____

_____

_____

I have the right to _____

I will assert this right by _____

_____

_____

_____

Creating Space

Defensiveness is an attempt to prevent or avoid uncomfortable emotions related to taking responsibility for one's actions. Defensiveness often gets in the way of healthy communication in times of conflict. It arises when our emotions become overwhelming and we have difficulty seeing clearly and putting things in perspective. Use this exercise to create space between yourself and your emotions so you can become less reactive.

1. **Slow down** and breathe.

2. **Bear witness** to the sensations in your body. Maybe it is an extreme tightness in your chest or lump in your throat.

3. **Let go of judgment** and simply explore the sensation with curiosity.

4. **Label the sensation** as best you can. For example, "This is fear in my chest" or "This is sadness in my throat."

5. **Remind yourself** that the emotion you are experiencing is a part of you and not all of you.

What emotions or situations trigger defensiveness within you? What are some behaviors or habits for which you have difficulty taking responsibility? Use this space to understand the intention behind those behaviors and healthy alternatives that are more consistent with your values.

PESSIMISM VS. OPTIMISM

Pessimism is the anticipation of bad things happening and viewing negative events as related to long-standing traits instead of situational explanations. Optimism anticipates positive things happening in the future and is associated with viewing negative events as related to situational factors and seeking out alternative explanations. Use the following table to identify your pessimistic viewpoints and rewrite them more optimistically, seeking out as many alternative explanations as you can before jumping to conclusions. An example is provided.

SITUATION	PESSIMISTIC VIEW	OPTIMISTIC VIEW
Example: My partner is home late from work.	*She's late because she is avoiding me and doesn't want to be with me anymore.*	*She could be late for a number of reasons. Maybe traffic was bad, or she got caught up in a meeting.*

Section 6
Reduce Stress and Calm Your Mind

In an attempt to bring tranquility or peace to your life, you might be tempted to avoid stressful situations or pain. Try not to discount your ability to manage stressful situations. We all have the innate ability to tolerate distress because we are built to feel emotions to help us survive. Without practice, we can easily abandon this skill and feel bombarded by overwhelming emotions in stressful events we aren't prepared for.

This section will help you reflect on and learn how to build your distress tolerance. The more confident you feel in your ability to handle stressful events, the less you will avoid them and lean on maladaptive habits or behaviors. This section will reinforce tools to manage stress, stay calm, and ground yourself so you can face stressful situations head-on.

Change does
not happen
right away.
This is why
growth is so
meaningful.

How well do you currently handle stressful situations? What is your current response? Are you more reactive or withdrawn? Reflect on how you currently respond to stressors in your relationships and note how well they align with your values. How might you change your response to be in better alignment?

_____

_____

_____

_____

_____

_____

_____

_____

_____

_____

_____

_____

_____

_____

_____

_____

Meditation for Letting Go

This meditation will help you release tension in your body and mind through relaxing visualizations to ease you into tranquility.

1. Find a comfortable, quiet place for undisturbed meditation.

2. With your eyes closed, visualize a burning candle (perhaps light a candle for reference). Feel the warmth of the flame on your skin as it heats and eases your body. Now picture wax gently dripping down the edge of the candle.

3. As the candle burns, the wax gently melts and eases its way all the way down to its base. Feel yourself melting into your seat, growing heavier, and releasing down to your base. Let your tension go just as the candle lets its wax go with its melting. Continue for several rounds of breath.

4. When you are ready, take a deep breath in. Blow out the visualized candle on the exhale. Open your eyes and reflect on the effects of your meditation practice.

How would your life look if you managed stressors differently? If certain things didn't bother you as much or you were less reactive to situations? Explore how your relationships with yourself and others would change. How might they grow stronger?

_____

_____

_____

_____

_____

_____

_____

_____

_____

_____

_____

_____

_____

_____

_____

_____

_____

Gratitude supports an attitude of compassion and connection. There is significant evidence to support the benefits of gratitude for mental health and well-being, so use this exercise to encourage your gratitude.

Pick a new idea, object, person, or place that you are grateful for each week, and use the calendar below to focus on how you can engage in activities that allow you to practice feeling gratitude.

	OCCASION FOR GRATEFULNESS EXAMPLE: I AM GRATEFUL FOR NATURE.	WEEK 1 GOAL:	WEEK 2 GOAL:
MONDAY	*I took a walk outside and actually smelled the flowers.*		
TUESDAY	*I ate dinner outside and enjoyed the breeze on my skin.*		
WEDNESDAY	*I went on a drive to a new area and took in the new scenery.*		
THURSDAY	*I went outside and meditated on my connection to nature for ten minutes.*		
FRIDAY	*I took a painting class that focused on nature.*		
SATURDAY	*I took a walk and recognized five new things in nature I appreciated.*		
SUNDAY	*I went to the botanical gardens and appreciated nature's beauty.*		

GET YOURSELF GROUNDED

Let's look at ways to ground yourself when you feel triggered. Go back to section 3 (page 39) and identify the triggers you try to avoid. As you may recall, exposure therapy includes grounding exercises and relaxation techniques. Use the following table to identify what grounding exercise works best when paired with a specific trigger. Then return to this table after testing out each grounding technique and make note of your results.

TRIGGER	GROUNDING TECHNIQUE	RESULT
Example: Feeling rejected.	Meditation for Letting Go (page 98).	My anxiety and distress started at an 8/10 and went down to a 5/10 after my first round of the meditation.

Grounding exercises are meant to bring you back down to earth when you are experiencing heightened emotions. They are designed to help you feel supported and rooted in yourself. Recall occasions in your life when you felt the most grounded in yourself. Describe these moments—who was there, and what was the situation? What themes can you notice? Identify what helps you feel secure.

Stressful situations, especially in relationships, are a part of life and bound to happen. Remember that stressors and conflict are evidence that a boundary has been crossed or neglected. Reflect on a past conflict or common stressor in your relationship and identify what boundaries are being crossed or pushed. How can grounding exercises help you stay present and respect those boundaries?

Gravitate toward Gratitude

When you're experiencing stress, it's easy to focus on what isn't going well or dwell on negative events in your life. There is actually a mental bias to focus on the negative—it's a protective mechanism to look out for dangerous situations that has stuck around from the prehistoric era, when life was much more physically dangerous and threats to our survival were more prevalent. However, this bias is no longer as protective as it once was, and we need to actively shift our perspectives to refocus on the positives.

Every day, focus on identifying three things you are thankful for or appreciate. It can be as simple as "I am thankful for a good night's sleep" or as complex as "I am thankful for relationships that push me to grow."

DE-STRESSOR CHECKLIST

Here is a helpful list of useful de-stressors to help you combat stress and anxiety. They range from physical objects to regular practices or behaviors. Check out the following list to see how many you currently use and maybe pick up a new de-stressor or two. Space is provided to add your own de-stressors, too, if there is anything else you find easy and relaxing.

☐ Weighted blanket: shown to reduce anxiety using deep pressure stimulation that can help reduce autonomic arousal

☐ Adult coloring books: shown to improve focus and enhance mindfulness

☐ Physical exercise: known to release endorphins and increase mindfulness

☐ Sleep: consistent and ample sleep aids in overall well-being

☐ Comedy: laughing stimulates circulation and aids in muscle relaxation

☐ Reaching out: connecting with others reminds you that you're not alone

☐ Other:

☐ Other:

☐ Other:

☐ Other:

4-7-8 BREATH WORK

Practicing breathing exercises combats the fight-flight-freeze stress response. It messages your body and brain that you are safe and combats the stress cycle from taking over your nervous system. This breathing exercise focuses on exhaling longer than you inhale to support your body's natural coping system, providing a sense of grounding.

1. Find a comfortable place to sit with your back straight.

2. Exhale your breath completely through your mouth, making a *whoosh* sound. Keeping your tongue at the top of your mouth near your front teeth and pursing your lips can help.

3. Now close your lips and inhale through your nose for a count of four.

4. Hold your breath for a count of seven.

5. Exhale completely through your mouth, making the same *whoosh* sound for a count of eight.

6. Repeat this cycle three more times.

When have you felt incredibly stressed and afterward realized thinking about the stressful situation was much worse than the actual situation? Often, the anticipatory anxiety is worse than the feared situation because we catastrophize or imagine the worst outcomes in our minds. Write about times your anticipatory anxiety has gotten the best of you and reflect on how you can reel it back in.

_____

_____

_____

_____

_____

_____

_____

_____

_____

_____

_____

_____

_____

_____

_____

_____

_____

At this point, you've learned a ton about codependency, triggers, and coping skills. Part of managing stress is remembering your goals and values. How can you combine the knowledge of codependency, your specific triggers, and new coping skills to better manage stressful situations? How have your goals from the start of this journal grown or shifted?

Remember that in a state of codependency, we don't have a good gauge of our own needs and desires because we have learned to prioritize the needs of others. In moments of stress, how can you check in with your needs? Use the following table to identify what you need in moments of stress and actions you can take to reduce stress and take care of yourself. An example is provided.

STRESSOR	MY NEED/DESIRE	ACTION TAKEN TO MEET NEED
Example: No one thanked me or seemed to appreciate the dinner I made.	To feel appreciated and respected by others.	Take a break for meditation and explore the cognitive distortions I am employing such as emotional reasoning. Repeat affirmations for self-appreciation.

Sometimes when we are overwhelmed, it stems from unmet needs that have built up over time, and one little stressor can push us over the edge. Regularly checking in with yourself and prioritizing your needs can prevent your stress from bubbling over. What are your current needs? Which ones are going unmet?

_____

_____

_____

_____

_____

_____

_____

_____

_____

_____

_____

_____

_____

_____

_____

_____

_____

Now journal about how you can schedule time in your life to consistently check in with yourself about these needs and better address them.

_____

_____

_____

_____

_____

_____

_____

_____

_____

_____

_____

_____

_____

_____

_____

_____

_____

_____

A Final Note

Congratulations on making it to the end of the journal. With time and consistency, you will learn to shift your focus to find even more balance within yourself and in your relationships.

Remember, the process of becoming aware of codependent traits, such as ignoring your needs, has taken time, so the process of unlearning such traits will take time too. Healing from codependency requires self-reflection and self-compassion. You're already off to a great start by using this journal and growing your self-awareness. So allow yourself to feel pride in taking the first and often the hardest step.

As you move foward, you have the power to change how you react when you feel triggered and to challenge your faulty perceptions. With practice you can learn to find more harmony in your relationships and overcome fears of being abandoned or rejected. By taking time to focus on yourself, you are creating the foundation for longstanding, balanced, and fulfilling relationships.

Thank you for opening yourself up to the pages of this journal. May you continue to find yourself and honor your needs in the challenges and triumphs to come.

Resources

Finding Help

Codependents Anonymous
Find local meetings and various resources to support you in healing from codependency at CoDA.org.

The National Hotline for Domestic Violence
This hotline provides free and confidential support for anyone experiencing domestic abuse. Call 1.800.799.SAFE (7233) or visit their website TheHotline.org. You can also text "START" to 88788 or contact via TTY (teletypewriter) at 1.800.787.3224.

Books

The Codependency Workbook: Simple Practices for Developing and Maintaining Your Independence by Krystal Mazzola. A comprehensive, CBT-based resource filled with research-based strategies and activities for people seeking to break out of their codependent patterns and reestablish boundaries.

Codependent No More: How to Stop Controlling Others and Start Caring for Yourself by Melody Beattie. An expert guide for codependents on how to stop controlling others and start caring for themselves.

How to Do the Work: Recognize Your Patterns, Heal from Your Past, and Create Your Self by Nicole LePera. A great overall resource for mental health and well-being.

Self-Love Workbook for Women: Release Self-Doubt, Build Self-Compassion, and Embrace Who You Are by Megan Logan. A self-care workbook with prompts, exercises, and affirmations to improve self-love.

Set Boundaries, Find Peace: A Guide to Reclaiming Yourself by Nedra Glover Tawwab. A *New York Times* bestseller that provides simple and effective ways to set healthy boundaries in relationships.

Podcast

Codependency No More Podcast by Brian Pisor. A podcast that explores codependency from a personal perspective along with conversations with experts and individuals with various points of view to help you in your journey to heal from codependency.

References

Ashdown, Brien K., Jamie S. Bodenlos, Kelsey Arroyo, Melanie Patterson, Elena Parkins, and Sarah Burstein. "How Does Coloring Influence Mood, Stress, and Mindfulness?" *Journal of Integrated Social Sciences* 8, no. 1 (2018): 1–21.

Beck, Aaron T. "Thinking and Depression: I. Idiosyncratic Content and Cognitive Distortions." *Archives of General Psychiatry* 9, no. 4 (1963): 324–333.

Benham, Grant. "Sleep: An Important Factor in Stress-Health Models." *Stress and Health* 26, no. 3 (2010): 204–214.

Bennett, Mary Payne, and Cecile Lengacher. "Humor and Laughter May Influence Health: III. Laughter and Health Outcomes." *Evidence-Based Complementary and Alternative Medicine* 5, no. 1 (2008): 37–40.

CoDA. "Am I Codependent? Co-Dependents Anonymous." May 2019. CoDA.org/wp-content/uploads/2020/07/Am-I-Co-Dependent-Bro -4002.pdf.

"Conflict: Definition & Meaning." *Merriam-Webster*. Accessed June 3, 2022. Merriam-webster.com/dictionary/conflict.

Cui, Ming, and Frank D. Fincham. "The Differential Effects of Parental Divorce and Marital Conflict on Young Adult Romantic Relationships." *Personal Relationships* 17, no. 3 (2010): 331–343.

Desmond, Tim. *Self-Compassion in Psychotherapy: Mindfulness-Based Practices for Healing and Transformation*. New York: W.W. Norton, 2015.

Duckworth, Angela. *Grit: The Power of Passion and Perseverance*. New York: Scribner, 2016.

Edenfield, Teresa M., and James A. Blumenthal. "Exercise and Stress Reduction." In *The Handbook of Stress Science*, edited by Richard J. Contrada and Andrew Baum. New York: Springer, 2011.

Ekholm, Bodil, Stefan Spulber, and Mats Adler. "A Randomized Controlled Study of Weighted Chain Blankets for Insomnia in Psychiatric Disorders." *Journal of Clinical Sleep Medicine* 16, no. 9 (2020): 1567–1577. Accessed June 3, 2022. Pubmed.ncbi.nlm.nih.gov/32536366.

Fischer, Judith L., and Lynda Spann. "Measuring Codependency." *Alcoholism Treatment Quarterly* 8, no. 1 (1991): 87–100.

Fosco, Gregory M., and John H. Grych. "Emotional, Cognitive, and Family Systems Mediators of Children's Adjustment to Interparental Conflict." *Journal of Family Psychology* 22, no. 6 (2008): 843–854.

Hur, Myung-Haeng, Ji-Ah Song, Jeonghee Lee, and Myeong Soo Lee. "Aromatherapy for Stress Reduction in Healthy Adults: A Systematic Review and Meta-analysis of Randomized Clinical Trials." *Maturitas* 79, no. 4 (2014): 362–369.

Jetten, Jolanda, Nyla R. Branscombe, S. Alexander Haslam, Catherine Haslam, Tegan Cruwys, Janelle M. Jones, Lijuan Cui, et al. "Correction: Having a Lot of a Good Thing: Multiple Important Group Memberships as a Source of Self-esteem." *PLoS One* 10, no. 6 (2015): e0131035.

Knudson, Theresa M., and Heather K. Terrell. "Codependency, Perceived Interparental Conflict, and Substance Abuse in the Family of Origin." *The American Journal of Family Therapy* 40, no. 3 (2012): 245–257.

Linehan, Marsha M., and Chelsey R. Wilks. "The Course and Evolution of Dialectical Behavior Therapy." *American Journal of Psychotherapy* 69, no. 2 (2015): 97–110.

Noriega, Gloria, Luciana Ramos, María Elena Medina-Mora, and Antonio R. Villa. "Prevalence of Codependence in Young Women Seeking Primary Health Care and Associated Risk Factors." *American Journal of Orthopsychiatry* 78, no. 2 (2008): 199–210.

Singh, Navreen K. "Does Colouring Promote Mindfulness and Enhance Wellbeing? A Randomised Controlled Trial." Doctoral thesis, University of Surrey (United Kingdom), 2018.

Taylor, Heidi Brunner. "Family-of-Origin Quality, Regulation of Negative Affect, Marital Stability, and Couple Drinking Patterns." Dissertation, Brigham Young University, 2006.

Weil, Andrew. "Three Breathing Exercises and Techniques." Last modified February 2022. Drweil.com/health-wellness/body-mind-spirit /stress-anxiety/breathing-three-exercises.

Acknowledgments

This book would not be possible without my clients' strength, vulnerability, and willingness to share their stories with me. Thank you to my friends and family and my loving partner, Tyler, for your endless support. Lastly, thank you to my editor, Adrian Potts, for your encouragement and helpful insights.

About the Author

 Kimberly Hinman received her PhD in counseling psychology from Columbia University. She is a licensed clinical psychologist practicing in Kansas City, Missouri, and New York, New York. She provides individual, couples, and family therapy as well as psychological and neuropsychological assessment. To learn more about Dr. Hinman, visit drkimberlyhinman.com